CURTAIN'S UP!

SECOND EDITION

SARAH JANE MARSCHNER

University of New Hampshire

Kendall Hunt
publishing company

Kendall Hunt
p u b l i s h i n g   c o m p a n y

www.kendallhunt.com
Send all inquiries to:
4050 Westmark Drive
Dubuque, IA 52004-1840

Copyright © 2001, 2011 by Sarah Jane Marschner

ISBN 978-0-7575-8572-2

Printed in the United States of America
10 9 8 7 6 5 4 3 2

WELCOME

The first rule of the theatre is that everyone has strengths that are needed in the theatre. . . . The jobs in the theatre are limitless and everyone can be used in a theatrical production.

This lab manual is to be used in an introductory course in theatre. At the University of New Hampshire, lectures are an integral part of the curriculum. The lectures are intended to introduce a broad picture of all aspects of theatrical production. Audience membership, acting, directing, design and construction, singing, dancing, stage and theatre management, and playwrighting are all part of the theatrical process. The lectures will describe all of these aspects of theatre in detail. However, theatre is an active and participatory art form, and the student of live theatre should become a part of as many of these activities as possible. This is the purpose of including lab work in this introductory course.

Lab time is devoted to hands-on work that will give the student an idea of what the production of a play involves. The work of the individual theatre artist will become clearer as the students become involved in the creative processes of these artists. It is also my fervent hope that the student will gain a new respect for the hard work of these theatre artists as they do the lab assignments.

But most of all, have fun!

Sarah Jane Marschner

CONTENTS

PART I

AUDIENCE MEMBERSHIP

Writing about a Theatrical Performance

Student evaluations of a theatrical performance should follow the guidelines of theatre criticism in general. It is important to keep in mind what a critic is supposed to accomplish when judging a theatrical performance. That is, to point out the good and bad points of a performance and make suggestions for improvement if appropriate. Negative and positive comments are valid if they are supported by facts and specific examples. The following guidelines will help in writing about a performance for this course.

Observation

The process of evaluating a theatrical performance starts off by attending that performance and observing every aspect of the play. Acting, directing, lighting, set design, costuming, audience membership, and the work of the playwright should all be taken into account. It is also important to read the program and the director's notes at this point in the process. Observation of the production is the first and most important part of the evaluation procedure.

Analysis

The next step in the process of the process is analysis. It is important to analyze what was in the production. This involves thought and recall and perhaps a little research. The program and director's notes should be on hand to refer to when analyzing the evening's production. All aspects of the production should be taken into consideration.

Such as:

✔ Lighting
✔ Acting (individual and ensemble performances)
✔ Set design
✔ Costuming
✔ Comfort of theatrical environment
✔ Direction (especially blocking)
✔ The script and its relationship to the actual production
✔ Choreography and music direction, if applicable
✔ Pre-show music, if applicable

All of these aspects affect the audience and their enjoyment of the show. They must all remain consistent to the director's overall concept in order to be believable to the audience. In the process of analysis, any inconsistencies become critical and worthy of mention in a review.

Evaluation

The last step in the process is one of evaluation. This occurs after attending the performance and carefully analyzing all aspects of play production that were observed. In this process, the individual production is often contrasted with other productions the reviewer has attended. The questions that follow should be answered as a part of this process. These questions will help in organizing all thoughts and impressions in preparation for writing the evaluative review.

Prescriptive reviews are reviews that give suggestions for any improvements or changes in the production. Novice reviewers might not feel qualified to make these suggestions . . . but they are, in reality, very well qualified to comment on what they have seen and considered. There are many examples of reviews that have made prescriptive suggestions and improved a production immeasurably. Organizing specific thoughts and suggestions can help the production of a new work.

Look over the following pages and make sure to fill in all of the information when writing your own review. Look back at the program and director's notes and be specific!

PART II

THEATRICAL REVIEW EXERCISES

NAME_____

ASSIGNMENT IN AUDIENCE MEMBERSHIP AND THEATRICAL CRITICISM

The space below is a worksheet for the papers that have been assigned in conjunction with your attendance at two theatrical productions. This additional information will be useful in writing your theatrical criticism.

1. What is the playwright's theme?

2. What information can be gathered from the director's notes?

3. Did you, as an audience member, attend this production with any preconceived ideas about the playwright, the script, or the production itself?

NAME_____

SPECIFIC QUESTIONS FOR A FORMAL REVIEW OF A PRODUCTION

1. What was the production attempting to do? (i.e. educate, highlight a historical time period, highlight a social or political issue, or perhaps to entertain)

2. Did the production meet these goals?

3. Was the attempt worth the effort?

4. List any suggestions that you might have that would help the production in meeting the goals that have been set.

NAME_____

ASSIGNMENT IN AUDIENCE MEMBERSHIP AND THEATRICAL CRITICISM

The space below is a worksheet for the papers that have been assigned in conjunction with your attendance at two theatrical productions. This additional information will be useful in writing your theatrical criticism.

1.   What is the playwright's theme?

2.   What information can be gathered from the director's notes?

3.   Did you, as an audience member, attend this production with any preconceived ideas about the playwright, the script, or the production itself?

NAME_____

SPECIFIC QUESTIONS FOR A FORMAL REVIEW OF A PRODUCTION

1. What was the production attempting to do? (educate, highlight a historical time period, highlight a social or political issue, or perhaps to entertain)

2. Did the production meet these goals?

3. Was the attempt worth the effort?

4. List any suggestions that you might have that would help the production in meeting the goals that have been set.

PART III

THEATRE HISTORY

THEATRE HISTORY

There are four basic movements in theatre history that are important to the study of live theatre. Each of these movements has a unique contribution to make in the formation of today's popular theatre.

THE GREEK AND ROMAN THEATRE

The Greek theatre is the foundation of all theatre, it is the birthplace of most theatrical traditions and terminology. Live theatre performances started as religious festivals to celebrate the manipulations of the Gods that were so important to Greek culture. The stories of the Gods were told by a chorus of actors who spoke and moved in unison. In a short time, individual actors would step forward and tell a part of the story alone. Soon these actors would assume characters within the story and acting as we know it today was born.

THE RENAISSANCE

During the 15th and 16th centuries a rebirth of the ancient Greek and Roman traditions spread throughout Europe. This included a renaissance of the ancient traditions of live theatre and some adaptations that helped create new theatrical traditions.

SHAKESPEAREAN OR ELIZABETHAN THEATRE

Queen Elizabeth I of England was a strong and vital leader of her people. She supported artists and found venues in which theatrical troupes could perform. All of the funds that were earned through royal performances were used to create public theatres, which were popular and extremely well attended.

The plays of this period divided into two main categories. The first, tragedies, stemmed from the Greek tradition of tragic heroes facing their fates. The second were comedies and they descended from the Roman tradition of earthy characters facing everyday comedic situations.

THE COMMEDIA DELL'ARTE

There was another form of theatre that thrived throughout Italy during the Renaissance. The Commedia Dell'Arte was touring theatre with actors that traveled to each small village in a wagon that could be converted to a stage. The actors of the Commedia were welcome visitors to each village and were subsidized by the village audiences.

The touring aspect of the Commedia Dell'Arte was not the only innovation of this time in Italy. The performances of this touring theatre were also almost entirely improvised. There were no scripts for these performances, only loosely organized stories that were recreated on the spot. The audiences were familiar with the basic plots of these touring plays and often joined in and portrayed characters during the performances.

The Commedia Dell'Arte gave us both touring and improvisational theatre, both of which are theatrical genres that are popular today.

THE COMEDY OF MOLIERE

Moliere, Jean Baptiste Poquelin, was a Renaissance playwright who was born into the court of Louis the Fourteenth of France. As a teenager he showed a remarkable talent for writing comic plays that ridiculed the courtiers and aristocrats that had been a part of his childhood. These plays were stinging in their condemnation of the governing institutions of the time. Moliere, and other playwrights of this day were responsible for the birth of satirical comedy, which is also quite popular in television and film and stage today.

THE TWENTIETH CENTURY

There are two remarkable theatrical innovations during the twentieth century, which lead us to present day and the theatre that we see today. Both of these innovations were fundamentally American and seem to have fit into the culture of the United States quite easily.

The first of these new theatrical genres is that of classic drama. The Greco-Roman and Elizabethan theatres produced classic tragedies that centered on a tragic hero that was superior to the common man in some way. Many of the plays that were written during the twentieth century are dramas in which tragic events happened to an average person. The tragic hero makes conscious decisions that lead to his downfall. In this way, twentieth century theatre audiences could have more empathy for the tragic situation because it quite literally happened to the "person next door."

The twentieth century also gave us the birth of musical theatre as we know it today. Musical theatre is a combination of music, movement and spoken dialog. All three of these elements are interdependent and each works to further the story being told. All three elements need to be a part of a musical theatre piece and each must work together with the other two facets of the production. Again, this is a truly American art form, which highlights the energy and creativity of that society.

NAME_____

ASSIGNMENT IN THEATRE HISTORY

We have studied many different eras in theatrical history. Each had its own style and each had its own unique language.
    In the space below write three versions of a four line scene in which two old friends meet after a short period of time and are glad to see each other. The first scene should be in the style of the Elizabethan theatre, the second in the style of the Commedia Dell'Arte and the third in musical theatre style.

PART IV

ACTING

WARM-UP EXERCISES FOR A LAB CLASS

The first rule of acting is that every actor must be clearly seen and heard when he or she is on stage.

Before each class begins, it is important for the entire group to participate in an activity that starts things off by involving everyone. Active theatre classes, like casts of a show, must develop a feel for working together and each actor should sense what the other members of the group are doing. All levels of performance depend on this group understanding.

Physical and vocal warm-ups will begin the class. Music (especially musical theatre music) helps set an active tone for the class. Basic dance movements can be included in these warm-ups and the vocal warm-ups approach singing. The warm-ups are uniquely fun and serve a definite theatrical purpose.

The group is now ready for more traditional theatre exercises with clear objectives. There are many published theatre games which will meet the desired objectives. The ones that follow are to be used as a starting point and are adaptable to many different situations.

THEATRICAL WARM-UP EXERCISES

Clap'a Your Hands

A group of six to eight students gather in a circle in the acting space. The leader starts off to the left and claps. The person to the left senses, without looking at the leader's hands (from peripheral vision, and the leader's eyes) the exact moment when the leader is going to clap. The person to the left then passes the clap on to the next person in the circle and it continues on until a rhythm is set within the group.

The object is for the two claps to happen at exactly the same time. This can only happen if the two people involved are really aware of each other and aware of the space. It is very important that actors on stage develop this awareness of each other and this exercise will heighten the awareness of both student actors and students in introductory theatre courses.

Two Balls and a Strike

In this exercise, six to eight students gather together in a circle. The leader throws an imaginary ball, with a corresponding sound, to any other member of the group. That person has to catch the imaginary ball and throw the next ball, with its corresponding sound. The leader is in control and decides when the balls should stop flying around.

The object of this exercise is for the participants to be attentive to the entire acting space and to be aware that the ball could be directed to them at any point. This requires concentration and an acute sense of observation. Vocal work is brought into the exercise by using appropriate sounds with each ball. Creativity in these sounds should be encouraged. The sounds and physicality of throwing the balls makes this a fun exercise for actors and students in introductory theatre courses.

Sit Down

In this exercise, six to eight students line up in the front of the acting space. The leader asks for a plot idea from any audience member. The leader may adapt this original subject in any way that might make it more interesting. The leader starts off by stating the first plot event and pointing to one of the students in the line. That person must supply the next plot event and stop when the leader points to another selected student. That student continues the story with the next event. If the student selected hesitates or repeats, the audience can tell them politely to sit down. This leads to the original group losing members and eventually leads to two people telling the story in alternating events. The end of the exercise comes when one "storyteller" is left standing and a champion is declared.

The object of this exercise is for students to be aware of the progression of a plot and the way in which the plot of a play builds. The story, as it is told in this exercise, should build as in good drama. In addition, the exercise will create a sense of verbal creativity in the class. These two objectives will benefit the cast of a play and an introductory class in theatre.

CHARACTER-CREATION EXERCISES

A script will give an actor all of the information that is needed. Each piece of information will help in the interpretation of character. Inflection, facial expression, physical movement, and tone of voice will all change to fit the situation that the characters are in according to the script. The following two short scenes will change with the two actors when the situation of the script changes. The lines remain the same, it is the director who changes the interpretation with the instructions that follow.

It's All in How You Look at It

One Man and One Woman

The lines:
1. I really thought you would come.
2. I told you I might not come.
1. I really thought you'd be there.
3. Sorry.
    a. The two characters are middle school students who were supposed to meet at the Friday dance. . . . The girl didn't show and the young man doesn't know why.

    b. The two characters are college students who were supposed to meet for a first date. Again, the gal didn't show up.

    c. The two characters were supposed to get married on Saturday. However, the bride wasn't there!

    d. The two characters live in a retirement home. . . . The gentleman had a visit from his family and he wanted to introduce them to his new friend.

Friends for Life

Two Women

The lines:
1. So, isn't he adorable?
2. I don't really think so.
1. You must be nuts!
2. He's fine, just not for me.
    a. Two characters are ninth graders who are talking about the new guy in class.

    b. The two characters are college roommates, one of whom has just come home from a blind date and the other who wants to hear the report from the date.

    c. The two characters are married moms who are talking about the husband of their new neighbor.

    d. The two characters are two elderly ladies who are talking about the new man at their bingo game.

THE HARDEST CONFESSION OF ALL

The lines:
1. I am really sorry.
2. What are you going to do now?
1. I'm not sure.
2. Figure it out.
    a. The two characters are a fifth grade teacher and his prize student and the young man didn't do his most important assignment of the semester.

    b. The two characters are father and son and the son cracked up the family car on his first solo drive.

    c. The two characters are boss and employee and the employee has not finished an important project.

Undecided

1. So, did you decide to go?
2. I'm not sure yet.
1. Everyone's going to be there.
2. Maybe I will.
    a. Two middle school kids in study hall talking about a dance

    b. A college party that seems to make the speakers uncomfortable

    c. Two yuppie friends who are talking about a neighborhood cocktail party

    d. Two elderly friends talking about going to Bingo

The Purchase

1. Have you got enough money?
2. I'm almost there.
3. Terrific, let's go shopping.
4. Not so fast.
    a. Two seventh graders are talking about going to a CD store

    b. Two college kids are talking about buying a new outfit for a party

    c. Two yuppie friends are planning redecoration of a living room

    d. Two thieves are talking about their latest mugging

NAME_____

CHARACTER DEVELOPMENT ASSIGNMENT

It's your turn. On this page you are to write a two-page scene of four lines. You are then to describe at least three situations in which these lines could be spoken. Include descriptive information of the characters involved in the scene.

Improvisational Theatre

To be "in character" simply means that an actor is speaking and moving as the character they are portraying. The actor must forget his own speech and natural movement.

Improvisational theatre is basically theatre without scripts. The elements of good acting are all involved in improvisation excluding the words of a playwright. An improvisational actor must listen to the words of all of the other actors and respond to all words and actions that happen within the scene. This response must be immediate, believable and consistent to the action of the scene.

Good improvisational acting is "thinking on your feet" and is actually more difficult than it appears. For this reason, students of acting usually begin with classes in improvisation in order to perfect the skills of listening and responding within a performance.

The role of a director in an improvisational scene is critical. The scene must be set with care. The number of actors, their age and gender, their physicality and their personality type may be taken into account by the director in setting up the improvisation. The audience may also be considered in the description of the initial conflict that starts off the improvisation.

An improvisation begins by the introduction of this initial conflict that exists between the characters that are involved in the improvisational scene. This outline of the scene will also include some basic information about the characters such as ages, professions, relationship with the other characters, and often personality traits which might affect the lines and action of actors. It is important that this conflict between characters involve a situation that can come to a natural completion so that the scene has a beginning, a series of middle events, and an endpoint. The actors should be aware that the conflict should be resolved by the end of the scene. Indeed, directors often allow the actors to decide upon the resolution of the conflict before improvising. This conversation between the actors will help in the flow of the scene and the development of the dialog.

The scene is set by the director and the actors have the basic information that they need. The improvisation is now ready to occur. It takes a great deal of skill to make dialogue sound realistic and smooth dialogue in an improvisation—it is much more difficult than it appears. Each actor must listen with care to what is being said. It is then essential to react "in character" to all that is happening on stage!

Improvisational Outlines

Improvisations usually involve dialogue between two or more people. It is also important to remember that good improv depends on conflict. In addition, character traits given to each cast member help to set the tone of the improv. The improv director must set the scene using these three starting points.

The following are ideas for scenes that introduce a conflict that can start off the improvisation. These ideas are broken down into number of cast members and gender of cast members for convenience. It is important to note that these are only a few ideas for improvisations and many other ideas can be added by the improvisation director.

IMPROVISATION FOR TWO CAST MEMBERS

One Man and One Woman

1. A twelve-year-old boy is waiting for his mom to come home. The young man has broken his principal's windshield during recess. The mother in the scene has had a great day at work. In the scene, the son has to tell his mother what has happened and the mom has to react to the story.
2. Two college students, a young man and a young woman, are in a pub. The woman is at the tavern with her friends who have left her temporarily. The man is at the pub alone, and is not a strong ladies man. He is trying hard to find a date. In the improvisaton, the man should, therefore, try and get the woman to go out with him and the woman should try and get the man to leave her alone.
3. A man runs a convenience store and is breaking in a new employee. This employee is not particularly work-oriented and doesn't want to hear all of the passionately offered instructions from the boss.

IMPROVISATION FOR TWO CAST MEMBERS

Two Women

1. Two roommates meet in their dorm room. One of the women has been dating a man named Fred. She has been home expecting a call from Fred to make plans for the upcoming weekend. Her roommate has been to the library and met Fred there. He asked her out and she told him she would have to receive her roommate's permission before she could accept. In the improvisation, the roommates have to work out their problems and decide if either of them is going out with Fred.
2. Two women are at the local mall. One is assigned the role of a saleslady, the other a shopper. The shopper brings out different outfits and the saleslady has to earn her commission by convincing her that each outfit is perfect and flattering.
3. A mom and her fourteen year old daughter are sitting at home. In this improvisation, the daughter has to get permission to go out on her first "car date" with her new boyfriend. The mother has shown in the past that she is not likely to approve.

IMPROVISATION FOR THREE CAST MEMBERS

Three Men

1. Three young customer service men are meeting in the break room of their office. They have been told that one of them is going to be promoted. The improvisation will center around their feelings toward the promotion and their chances of being chosen.
2. Three hockey players have been informed that there is a girl who has been accepted on their team. During the conversation, the emotions and attitudes toward this new member should be become clear.

IMPROVISATION FOR THREE CAST MEMBERS

Three Women

1. Three women are gathered together in the waiting room of a publishing company. They each discuss what they have written and why it should be published. The conversation should center around the value of their work. An option could be to have the class decide, by vote, which piece is published.
2. This improvisation takes place in a classroom. The teacher has called in two mothers whose children were involved in a pushing incident on the playground. It would be interesting if each mother could show a different attitude towards the meeting.

GENERAL IMPROVISATION FOR THREE OR MORE CAST MEMBERS

1. This improvisation takes place in an eighth grade classroom. The hardest group of students in the school are waiting for their fourth substitute of the year. Another cast member is sent in to assume the role of the teacher. The rest of the improvisation centers around the reaction of the kids and the reaction of the teacher to their behavior. All thrown paper airplanes need to be picked up at the end of class.
2. A biochemistry class is the center of this improvisation. A quiz is being given in class and the teacher has left the room. Two of the students have not studied for this quiz at all. These students are seated on either side of a third student who knows the quiz material and has studied extensively. The two outside students want the third to allow them to cheat on the quiz and the middle student is not likely to share his hard work with them.
3. This improvisation takes place in a large local grocery store. The first character that appears is a prize winning cashier who is in charge of a "twelve or under" line. Different characters appear, such as:
   a. A woman who has forty items to check out and wants to pay with a check
   b. A mother who has to get home for her four year old's birthday party and only wants to buy some candles
   c. A young man who has invited his date over for dinner and doesn't know how to boil water
   d. A gourmet chef who is looking for some obscure ingredients for a difficult recipe
4. The scene of this improvisation is set at a retirement home. A group of the residents meet every afternoon on the back porch to swap stories of the day. A new resident, who is already disliked, enters the scene and disrupts the conversation. He or she is a character who doesn't listen to anyone else and is not concerned with their stories. An additional character might enter the scene who could portray a nurse to break up the conversation and send everyone to dinner.

MONOLOGUES

Monologues are speeches of length that are delivered to one other character or delivered directly to an audience by an actor alone on stage.

This section of the manual is devoted to monologue that can be delivered in class or used for audition purposes. Professional actors always have classic, current, comedic, and dramatic monologues at their disposal. For this reason, the monologues chosen are from classic comedies and tragedies. There are also two current monologues written for today's university students. These monologues will be used in class and dissected through discussion.

BLIND DATE

Monologue for a Young Man

Okay, so I'll never go on a blind date again . . . I've never liked blind dates before so I don't know why I thought this one would be any different.

It all started when one of the guys on the floor asked me if I would double with him and his current girl. He said his girl had one of her high school friends coming into town for the weekend and she would only keep her Saturday date if he could find someone for the friend. I wasn't going to go, but he had done me a couple of favors and I felt like I had to. What a pain in the neck. I should have known better.

I was all ready to go but Jim, my friend, took his usual three hours in front of the mirror and it got to be quite late. I tried to hurry him up, but he's a real jerk and just took some more time with his hair. Finally the girls called and so he moved along. We couldn't find a parking space in front of the girl's dorm so I had to go in and tell them we had arrived. Jamie, Jim's girl, is an OK girl and I like her, so as I walked to her door I thought things might work out all right. Jim had told me that Becky, my date, was cute and full of personality so I was ready to meet her. When she opened the door I was kind of surprised because she really was cute.

But things went downhill from there. As we were walking to the car, my date started to go on and on about how exciting our campus was and how many hunky guys she had seen. RIGHT, just what a guy wants to hear. Then we got in the car and she spent four miles telling us about some dumb chick flick that she had just seen. It was a definite case of who cares. Some stupid boy meets girl, girl gets boy, they end up happy and that's about it kind of story. She said she'd really love to see it again after dinner. Jim and I just ignored the hint and went into the restaurant. Now things got really bad—the girl ate like she hadn't had a meal in a month. She ordered everything on the menu and didn't look at the price. I leaned over to Jim and told him I hoped he had brought his ATM card.

During dinner this girl told the story of her life. She was the prom queen at her high school and she was voted best smile in her class. I wanted to tell her that you couldn't prove it by me since she hadn't smiled once since I met her. I couldn't help thinking that I was giving up a hockey game with my buddies for all this. But Jim and Jamie were having a good time so I decided to tough it out.

It wasn't easy though. Becky didn't want to hear about anything interesting. I tried to talk to her about the hockey game and I hoped she'd get interested and want to go. She said that hockey was too violent. I started to tell her about this theatre course I am taking and that is always good for a laugh, but she said that she loved the theatre and thought it was the most important course anyone can take. I thought she might be impressed when I told her I was a chemical engineering major; something had to work with this girl. She told me that all of that engineering stuff was too much for her artistic brain.

The girls went to the bathroom and by the time they got back it was clear that we were going to take them back to their dorm and call it a night. They kept talking about all of these ridiculous things that they wanted to do when they got home.

Now I'm a pretty good guy, not hard to get along with. But for the life of me I will never understand women. You try to be nice and kind and they make you feel like a weirdo. I listened to this girl all night and tried real hard to be interested in what she was saying, and she just kept on talking.

I can tell you this much though. This is absolutely the last blind date I will ever go on in my life?

Monologue for a Young Woman

Okay, so I'll never go on a blind date again. I never liked blind dates before so I don't know why I thought this one would be any different.

It all started when I decided to visit my friend Jamie at her college. I want you to understand I turned down two dates just to go. Jamie said her boyfriend Jim would get me a Saturday night date and we would double for dinner and whatever. I've met Jim and I like him so I thought it would all work out fine. You know, any friend of Jim's is a friend of mine. Boy, was I wrong. First off, Jim and his friend Brian were an hour late to pick us up. We were ready to go and we had to just sit there and wait. Finally, Jamie called over there and told them to get moving.

Brian came and got us and when we were walking to the car I just casually mentioned how great the campus was. I wanted to make the guys feel comfortable so I happened to mention that there were lots of cute guys around. This seemed to irritate Brian, although I have no idea why. On the ride to the restaurant I was searching to find something to talk about, so I mentioned this wonderful movie I had seen. It is one of those tear-jerking romantic movies that is a perfect date movie. Again, nobody seemed interested. Finally we got to the restaurant and I was pleased. It was an

Italian restaurant and that's my absolute favorite food. I ate my meal and could have eaten a lot more, too, but my mother always told me not to make a pig of myself on a date. During dinner Brian took up the whole conversation. He talked about hockey. I mean really, I can't stand all of the hitting and checking stuff. Then he made fun of his theatre course. I quickly told him that theatre was cool and I hoped that would make him shut up. No such luck. Then the arrogant jerk started pulling the chemical engineering routine just so I would be impressed. Anyone could study chemical engineering—anyone. I was definitely not impressed. When we ordered dessert I got Jamie to go to the bathroom with me and I just told her that it was over and that I wanted to go back to the dorm and hang out. She didn't want to upset Jim and disappoint Brian, but we decided to try and end the evening.

When we got back to the table, we kept dropping hints about doing nails and studying and looking at pictures in our high school yearbook. The guys got the hint and took us home. It was a relief to have the horrible evening over.

Now, I am a pretty nice girl, and not hard to get along with. But for the life of me, I will never understand men. You try and be polite and keep the conversation going. I tried all night to talk about stuff this guy would be interested in, and he just wasn't interested.

I can tell you this, though, this is absolutely the last blind date I will ever go on in my life.

NAME_____

MONOLOG ASSIGNMENT

You are to write a monolog (and have it memorized) about your first year in college. There are examples to follow, which will help you in creating your monolog.

PART V

SCENES

Aristophanes

LYSISTRATA: In the last war we were too modest to object to anything you men did—and in any case you wouldn't let us say a word. But don't think we approved! We knew everything that was going on. Many times we'd hear at home about some major blunder of yours, and then when you came home we'd be burning inside but we'd have to put on a smile and ask what it was you'd decided to inscribe on the pillar underneath the Peace Treaty. —And what did my husband always say?—'Shut up and mind your own business!' And I did.

Lysistrata: But sure enough, next thing we knew you'd take an even sillier decision. And if I so much as said, 'Darling, why are you carrying on with this silly policy?' he would glare at me and say, 'Back to your weaving, woman, or you'll have a headache for a month. "Go and attend to your work; let war be the care of the menfolk."'

We should not be allowed to make the least little suggestion to you, no matter how much you mismanage the City's affairs? And new, look, every time two people meet in the street, what do they say? 'Isn't there a man in the country?' and the answer comes, 'Not one.' That's why we women got together and decided we were going to save Greece. What was the point of waiting any longer, we asked ourselves. Well now, we'll make a deal. You listen to us—and we'll talk sense, not like you used to—listen to us and keep quiet, as we've had to do up to now, and we'll clear up the mess you've made.

THE TEMPEST

PROSPERO: Ye elves of hills, brooks, standing lakes, and groves,°
And ye that on the sands with printless foot
Do chase the ebbing Neptune, and do fly him
When he comes back; you demi-puppets° that
By moonshine do the green sour ringlets° make,
Whereof the ewe not bites; and you whose pastime
Is to make midnight mushrooms,° that rejoice
To hear the solemn curfew,° by whose aid,
Weak masters though ye be, I have bedimmed
The noontide sun, called forth the mutinous winds,
And twixt the green sea and the azured vault°

Set roaring war; to the dread rattling thunder
Have I given fire,° and rifted,° Jove's stout oak
With his own bolt;° the strong-based promontory
Have I made shake, and by the spurs° plucked up
The pine and cedar; graves at my command
Have waked their sleepers, oped, and let 'em forth
By my so potent art. But this rough° magic
I here abjure, and when I have required°
Some heavenly music—which even now I do—
To work mine end upon their senses that°
This airy charm° is for, I'll break my staff,
Bury it certain fathoms in the earth,
And deeper than did ever plummet sound
I'll drown my book.
   (Solemn music.)

42

A MIDSUMMER NIGHT'S DREAM

PUCK: If we shadows have offended,
Think but this, and all is mended,
That you have but slumb'red here°
While these visions did appear.
And this weak and idle theme,
No more yielding but° a dream,
Gentles, do not reprehend.
If you pardon, we will mend.
And, as I am an honest Puck,
If we have unearned luck
Now to scape the serpent's tongue,°
We will make amends ere long;
Else the Puck a liar call.
So, good night unto you all.
Give me your hands,° if we be friends,
And Robin shall restore amends.

The Misanthrope

ALCESTE
Well, what's better, showing false affections?
Groveling in social genuflections?
Those oily "thee and thou" words, how I hate 'em!
And flatterers and cowards: Heaven grate 'em
Into shreds!
With all their vile pretensions in their heads!
Those stuck-on-smiling, so-beguiling faces!
Those amorous, gregarious embraces!
Those horribly inflated salutations
That lead to more exalted protestations!
Why should I care if a man speaks me well,
When I am just one of his vast clientele?
Why soak up flattering praises from one
who equally flatters ALL UNDER THE SUN!
Ah no, Philinte, I'm one who quite abhors
The flatteries of social snobs and bores.
Give me a friend who's mind is still his own—
Who'll give his love to ME, and ME ALONE!
If words or praise are those that will be heard,
Why, then I—dammit!—want to be PREFERRED,
Not mixed among the lot of common men!
Well, then, Philinte: what's YOUR position then?
Do you prefer ME to that simpleton?
The man who loves ALL men cannot love ONE!

SERVANT OF TWO MASTERS

TRUFFALDINO: Later, eat later! How many times must I swallow the word "later" before I finally choke on my pride? How much more can I take? If I knew where my master was going to stay, I could beg a bite on credit . . . But no! My master leaves his bags on the dock, me on the street, and my stomach with nothing to feed on but anger. (holds his stomach) What? I know, my darling. If I could just find the smallest opportunity to make a few lira, then I can put some food into you . . . What? . . . Where! (stomach turns him around) I'll give him a try, my darling!

PART VI

DIRECTING

THE PROCESS OF DIRECTING

The first rule of directing is that a director is involved in every aspect of a play's production and is the final decision maker in every dispute.

The process of directing is difficult, time consuming and all-encompassing. There are many ways in which a director is put together with a theatrical piece. These routes have been discussed in class. We shall begin this section by assuming that director and script have been assigned to each other. We can also assume that all of the theatrical artists are completely familiar with the script before the process begins. The director then starts by developing a director's concept. This is a total vision for the production that involves all aspects of a production. The director must make sure that all of the elements remain consistent with the total concept.

All of the following elements are taken into account when forming a director's concept. This is only a partial list of what the director must consider when directing a show.

✔ Costuming
✔ Make-up
✔ Marketing of the production
✔ Program and director's notes
✔ Casting
✔ Blocking
✔ Lighting
✔ Set design
✔ Set construction

A good director is a combination of visionary, artist, and down-to-earth workhorse. The director must be creative and practical. The director must also have the ability to put the production's concept into words that are concise and specific. All of the other theatrical artists need to understand this concept and be able to make the adjustments that are necessary for the specific production.

NAME_____

ACTIVITIES FOR DIRECTING

The following assignments will deal with the work of the director in the beginning stages of the director's work.

1. In the space below write a twelve to eighteen line dialogue that introduces two characters discussing a job that they really want. Include lines that describe the job and lines that tell the audience why the job is important.

2. Write your short dialogue over in the space provided and add stage directions that give the director and actor more information. The stage directions should help in interpretation of lines and in blocking.

3. Describe, in your own words, the stage picture for your short scene. Include set design, colors, fabrics, props and general style of what the acting space should look like.

PART VII

PLAYWRIGHTING

THE ART OF PLAYWRIGHTING

The art of playwrighting is often a solitary one. The playwright creates alone and is unaware of how the script is going to work in front of an audience.

There are certain limitations that a playwright takes into consideration from the start. The playwright is limited in scope in many ways. The first is the limitation of time. The playwright must assume that there is a limitation of about three hours in which to tell the complete story of the script. Audiences will remain attentive for about that amount of time and any longer than that will cause a loss of attention.

The second limitation of time concerns the "world of the play" time that is covered in the script. Most scripts cover a span of weeks or months, not years or decades. This is because most actors could not believably age without lengthy costume and make-up work.

Another limitation that must be considered in the initial stages of writing is a limitation of space. The playwright must be aware that all of the action of the play must take place within the confines of a typical acting space. Visions must often be altered to fit the confines of a stage. An elephant must be described because it cannot be brought on the stage. The action of the play cannot take place in Athens and move abruptly to Antarctica. The number of settings and scene changes has to be limited within the script so that the play can be produced by many different groups.

It is also important for the playwright to address limitations in terms of characterization. The characters must be clearly defined in terms of motivation. Audiences need to understand the reasons behind the action and dialogue for each character. Clearly defined motivation will help hold the interest and involvement of the audience.

All of these limitations are important for the playwright and become second nature with experience. However, the most important skill in playwrighting is the use of common sense. We know that believability and consistency are essential guidewords for all theatre artists, and this begins with the playwright. The world of the play must be believable and the script must remain true to the story being told or the play won't work in front of an audience. Playwrights know this instinctively and will adjust their script to eliminate all action and dialogue that is untrue or inconsistent.

THE PLAYWRIGHTING PROJECT

The playwrighting project is one of the most extensive assignments that this course offers. It involves group work and cooperative effort. In this way, it is different from the work of an individual playwright who works alone. A great deal of class time will be spent on working together as a group and coming up with a successful script. The culmination of the project is the presentation of the group's script to the rest of the class. The performances should last from about six to ten minutes and can be read aloud from the scripts.

The process involved in this project is going to be carefully outlined. Each step is designed to help complete the project, and have some fun along the way.

STEP ONE

The students will arrange themselves in groups of eight or less. This project works well when students don't know each other and the groups becomes diverse.

STEP TWO

In this step, the group starts the brainstorming process. The first task is to compile a list of the names of all group members. A copy of this list is to be handed in for attendance.

STEP THREE

The group then begins to discuss ideas for their six to ten minute scenes. The following guidelines will help:

1. It is a good idea to look at the group members and find an idea that includes them all, according to age and gender. This is because it is always easier to write about characters that are familiar to the beginning playwright.
2. It will be easier for the groups to write in the genre of comedy. It is a bit easier to come up with actual dialogue and will be more enjoyable for the class to watch in performance. Comedy is also less intimidating for the budding actor to present in performance.
3. The entire scene should be based on some conflict in characters. It is crucial that the individual characters are in some sort of conflict with each other. This is the foundation for all good drama and is important for audience interest. The characters should want something different from each other or from the situation.
4. Each scene should present a clear plot with a solid beginning, interesting events in the rising action, a climax, and a clear resolution to the conflicts (a beginning, a middle and an end). All audiences want to see events resolved; they don't want to be left up in the air!
5. Every idea should be considered. Each member of the group should feel free to present a possible subject.

STEP FOUR

This step involves the actual writing of the script. (Remember, this is not improvisation, a script will be passed in!) The key words of believability and consistency enter into this phase of the project. The lines written should reflect realistic dialogue that sounds as if the words are true to the characters involved. Each member of the group should contribute to the brainstorming. A secretary should be elected so that the lines can be written down to form a script.

STEP FIVE

There should be a rehearsal of the script which will help the flow of lines when the script is read aloud in class. Everyone should be familiar with the responsibilities involved and practice will help. At this point, the group will discuss any props that need to be gathered and brought to class. It may also be appropriate to decide on simple costume pieces that will help define the different characters in the production. The characters and their personality traits can be more clearly defined by simple costumes and certain props.

NAME_____

PLAYWRIGHTING PROJECT WORKSHEETS

1. Names of the members of the group

2. Basic outline of the plot

3. Describe your character

4. Any props that need to be brought to the performance

5. Description of costumes that will be worn

PART VIII

MUSICAL THEATRE

MUSICAL THEATRE

A musical theatre is the telling of a story to an audience using song and dance and script. All the elements of the piece fit together to tell one complete story.

Music is universal and adds to the audience enjoyment of the play.

THE BEGINNINGS (1800S–1934) THE EARLY PATRIOTS

Musical theatre has many forms of entertainment that are combined to make musical plays as we know them today

(a) opera (music)
(b) ballet (dance)
(c) non-musical plays (script)
(d) minstrel shows
(d) variety shows or vaudeville

Each of these entertainments had elements of musical theatre, but did not combine all the elements into telling one story.

The first piece of musical theatre which was written as such was *LITTLE JOHNNY JONES* (1904), music and lyrics and script by George M. Cohan. The early musical theatre shows were patriotic and very American in their energy and presentation. Composers such as Irving Berlin and Jerome Kern were a part of this growing trend.

THE ROMANTICS (1934–1943)

Many composers and lyricists were part of the early patriots but also wrote musicals that were romantic and opulent. These shows were a direct reaction to The Great Depression of 1929. They were designed to show people a better life and inspire them. Cole Porter and George and Ira Gershwin were a part of this trend.

THE GOLDEN AGE OF MUSICAL THEATRE (1943–1959)

Most of the musical plays that we all know come from this era.

The name "Golden Age" indicates that money was important to the theatre of this time

- ✔ Musical plays brought in larger audiences.
- ✔ Musical plays had longer first runs in their initial productions.
- ✔ Tangent products were sold in conjunction with these musical plays.
- ✔ The rights to perform these plays were given to outside groups worldwide.
- ✔ The musical plays of this time had universal themes, which appealed to large audiences.
- ✔ Richard Rodgers and Oscar Hammerstein (OKLAHOMA, THE SOUND OF MUSIC) and Alan J. Lerner and Fritz Loewe (MY FAIR LADY, CAMELOT) were important composers and lyricists of this time.

THE MODERN ERA (1964–THE PRESENT)

With the opening of the play *Hair*, each musical play brought something unique to the audiences.

- ✔ There were different styles of music and dance used in these plays. (especially, rock and roll and jazz and blues)
- ✔ There was a rebirth of extravaganzas and very small musical plays during this period.
- ✔ Performers in recent years have to be proficient in acting, movement, and singing to assume roles in modern musical plays.
- ✔ Lord Andrew Lloyd Webber (*The Phantom of the Opera*), Schoenberg (*Les Miserables*) and John Kander and Fred Ebb (*Chicago and Cabaret*) were major contributors to musical theatre in the recent years.

NAME_____

ASSIGNMENT IN MUSICAL THEATRE

We have heard and seen many scenes and songs from different musicals of different times. Which one was the most interesting and enjoyable to you, and why?

PART IX

TECHNICAL THEATRE

TECHNICAL THEATRE

The term technical theatre involves many aspects of a theatrical production; this includes sets, lights, costumes, makeup, and props.

All technical theatre artists have some basic things in common; included in this are two facets of technical artistry, design, and construction. In most cases, the person who designs the set does not build it, the person who designs the lighting plan does not hang the lights, and the costume designer will often not sew the costume. All designs are approved by the director before the construction is begun. All designers take four elements into account:

1. line
2. balance
3. texture
4. color

These four elements are a part of the set, lighting, costume, and makeup design. Sets are the most visible part of what the audience sees; therefore, all other technical elements must coordinate with the set design. The technical aspects of a theatrical production are the only part of a theatrical production budget where expenses can be cut, and good designers are experts in saving money. Technical theatre artists work behind the scenes and often do not get credit for their hard work.

NAME_____

ASSIGNMENT IN TECHNICAL THEATRE

Please define the following technical terms that are used in the lecture:

a) wings

b) proscenium stages

c) fly space

d) sets

e) flats

f) backdrops and cycloramas

NAME_____

SECOND ASSIGNMENT
IN TECHNICAL THEATRE

You are the technical designer for a play about your college life. Describe the sets and costumes in your design in the following ways:

LINE

BALANCE

TEXTURES

COLORS

PART X

THE FINAL PROJECT

NAME_____

THE FINAL COURSE PROJECT

The final project for this course is quite open-ended. The only restriction is that any activity that you select should reflect your interests and your personal strengths. There will be opportunities to plan and refine your project idea.

     The following is a list of questions that will help you in deciding on a final project idea, and will help outline the form of the project.

1.   What are you good at? What are your academic strengths?

2.   What aspect of theatrical production has been the most interesting and challenging for you?

3.   Where can you see yourself in terms of theatrical production? What aspect of production would you choose to become involved in?

NAME_____

HANDOUT FOR THE FINAL PROJECT

In the space provided below outline your final project idea. Include all information that will help describe what you want to accomplish. In addition, add information that will explain how this project is specifically designed for you as a theatrical artist.